ARTICULATED THOUGHTS

By Lauren K. Rodriguez

Copyright © 2015
Lauren Rodriguez
Frisco, Texas

Tribute Publishing

Articulated Thoughts
First Edition September 2015

All Worldwide Rights Reserved
ISBN: 978-0-990-6001-8-3

All Rights Reserved. No part of this book may be reproduced, stored in a retrieval system, or transmitted, in any form, or by any means, electronic, recorded, photocopied, or otherwise, without the prior written permission of the copyright owner, except by a reviewer who may quote brief passages in a review.

Printed in the United States of America.

For my friends & family

who encouraged thought.

TABLE OF CONTENT

Summer 1

Fall 61

Winter 111

Spring 151

Summer 165

I never intended for these poems to be read.

They are written chronologically, starting from the summer before my senior year at Baylor University, and ending the summer before my first year at Seminary. Inside you'll find poems of joy, heartache, growth, prayer, and nonsense; a year of my life from the perspective of poetry.

In the summer of 2014 I bought *No Matter the Wreckage* by Sarah Kay and fell in love with her writing, so much so that she gave me a voice. So that's where this book starts, after I bought her poetry book.

Lauren

Summer

HEY LOOK
I GOT A NEW POETRY BOOK

Isn't it funny

How life is so universally the same

And incumbently different

That a stranger's words could so very easily reflect my heart

Manifest themselves with such clarity that I didn't even know existed

And I find myself a little more

With the aid of a stranger

WHEN YOU FIND A NEW THING THAT'S UNIQUELY YOURS

Tonight was a night to sit at the top of a parking garage

Just go because you can, and the time is there and you are young and I

I can taste the air

It tastes of sighs and harmonies and peace

And the pretending is gone

From up here

Because there's no one to pretend for

And this moment is mine, and

I've never felt so refreshed and self-assured

This is who You've made me to be

I pray for others

I pray for the one {again}

I give thanks and rejoice in singing

You are my hope

And it's been restored

I can never pay You back

Except to love You evermore

WHEN MAKING CAREER CHOICES

Is procrastination

An aversion to working

Or to

The

Work

ON WHY I HAVE BEEN STOCKING UP ON REST

Sometimes

You have to stop

And smell the roses

Other times

You need to keep moving

And trust that there will be roses

Along the way

DEAR DAD

I forgive you for the thing you said that was offensive that I found out later was not offensive

ON DEATH & DYING

Is it weird

That I find comfort

That we're all going to die anyway

It makes the bad things not matter

And the good seem all the more significant

ON DEATH & DYING PART II

If death is just a cessation of valuable activity

Then I want to know what your activities are

Can we do them together?

The people who partake in activities

They perceive as not valuable

Are unhappy

Dead.

Luckily,

Mine is spending time

With people like you

And hoping

We both end up better for it

BLACKSMITH

I want to be a physician

So that after people see me

They leave better than when I found them

'How narcissist!' they grunt

'To believe others are enriched solely by your presence'

To say that is to imply that I am the blacksmith

When I'm really just the hammer

I don't serve because I can give

But so others can gain

I'm not the storehouse of knowledge

But the bridge to wisdom

Not a jar of preserves

But a faucet for water

Never depleted

But a temporary space

For an eternal love

ESSENTIAL BUILDING BLOCKS FOR A WOMAN GROWING INTO HERSELF

I feel happiest

When I can articulate my thoughts

And know they are exactly my own

That this new thought generated

Is added to the collection

Of who I am

And it will stick

Because I am stubborn

But also because I am consistent

And I like who I am

I am proud of who I am

When I draw my own, new conclusions

And know those thoughts are pleasing to You

And someday

They'll be pleasing to someone else, too

But until then

I'll delight in these thoughts

That I was able to articulate

Because one day

I'll articulate them to you

And you will like {most of} them

And then I'll hear

Your articulated thoughts, too

LEARNING TO LISTEN

The Lord gave me clarity,

In a church I don't like.

Of course.

He works like that, you know,

Giving love when we can only remember hate,

Giving strength when once before we felt weakness,

Giving peace when we had only tasted uneasiness.

The Lord gave me clarity:

Listen

Obey

Trust

He will act

Submit

He's in control

Be genuine

And the most genuine kind of person

Isn't trying to be genuine at all

You become the person you're meant to be when you aren't looking

AWKWARD SOCIAL ETIQUETTE

I forgot to call you back

One of those minor, run-of-the-mill,

"I'll call you back!" phone calls.

So, in embarrassment, I figured a political way

To explain

How I forgot you.

But how can you explain to someone,

That they weren't important enough to be remembered?

Alas,

I wasn't in a place to make a proper phone call,

And by the time I made it to a proper phone call place,

I forgot again.

How do you explain to someone,

That they weren't important enough to be remembered twice?

So, in embarrassment,

I put off the phone call

The cycle repeated

Days passed

We may never speak again

It's quite dramatic, really

Damn telephones

RULE #13

It's quite easy

To become his dream girl,

(Developing those quirks he'll adore

Impressing him with your talents

Sharing in your passions

Indulging him in your hobbies

Letting him fall in love with every drop of you

Until he is drowning,

Willingly)

When you're not trying to be his dream girl.

RULE #12

It's quite easy

To find your dream boy,

(The one who will throw rocks at your window

Have a passion for life

Will walk humbly

Lead well

And sing right along with you)

When you're not looking.

ON THE RULE NUMBERING

Because it would be just like life

To give you your dream boy

Before you were his dream girl

SOCK WARS

I like to sleep

With two socks on

And see which ones

Survive 'til morning

ON THAT LAST ONE

Hey

They can't all be winners

DISCIPLINE

I changed my password

To 'discipline'

But instead of motivation

I found guilt and

Disappointment

CONVERSATIONS

That moment

When a word is on the tip of your tongue

When you can smell; not taste

The fleeting thought you thought you had

That moment

When if you could just remember that word

Then they could understand.

That moment, (if it had a word)

Is my sworn enemy

It holds me back from displaying my ideas

Gesturing like Vanna

Allowing the conversationers to take a peek

To open the book

And hear the crack of the spine

Of the ideas I wish for them to hear

And if I can't find those words…

Then how are we to build anything?

Because that's what conversations do;

They build.

If I can artfully paint you a picture

Of what I mean to say

You get a glimpse of who I am

What my opinions are

My educational background

Where I'm from

And then you

You share yours

And I get a glimpse of you

Neither of us will know just exactly what the other will say

(which is what makes this part so beautiful)

So we begin to build

One first, then the other

Ideas flowing, thoughts shared

[Each conversation building its own unique thing]

Some build shelters:

Blocking themselves off,

keeping each other safe,

allowing the room to close off until they're breathing in the same air they've breathed out

and they don't know it but that's exactly what they hoped for but

nothing close to what they wanted

Some build castles

Glittering, dazzling things that harbor hope and childhood and nostalgia for things to come

Is it possible to be nostalgic for things that never happened?

And some build weapons

Big ones that can kill thousands,

and small ones that can just barely bruise the skin

but still hurt

most of the time almost just as much because

the other end of the ammunition

was a hand that once touched them with love

Creating an aura of war because something they once built turned sour,

maybe more than once

Some build dynasties

Exchanging hypothesis,

generating low-rumbling 'hmms' until the things they've built

have become this massive thing that now others can build off of, too

My favorite kind

Builds a pillow

Something soft to rest a head on

Breeds an absent-minded smile except when I'm looking right at it

Then the smile is with my whole face

Up close it has no meaning, each thread a nonsensical, singular thought

But when we step back

And look at this thing we've built

Together

We're comforted to find that

No one person has ever built something this beautiful

 Alone

PRACTICING RIGHTEOUSNESS

"Be careful not to practice your righteousness in front of others to be seen by them. If you do, you will have no reward from your Father in heaven."
Matthew 6:1

The Bible stresses to do the right thing

Even when no man is watching

I believe it's to show

That our faith is genuine

To do what we need to do to please God

When only God is there

That's hard to do

But it gets easier

And this foundation is our core self

We puff it up when others are around

But when bad things happen

The excess is scraped off

Like the indulgent finger of a child knifing the icing off a cake

When bad things happen

We go back to the core

That we built

While we were doing the right things

When no man was watching

And hope that next time

Our core is even stronger

WALLET

I like that song

Because it artfully displays

The fleeting collisions

Of contrasting lives

And how other people

And small moments

Can be made magical

Through a lyrical mess

HIS ONE JOB

I like how

In that one movie

That one photographer

Sometimes wouldn't take pictures

So as to not spoil the moment

It makes sense

In an ineffable way

MOVEMENT

"What happened here?"

"Movement"

That answer

Was my favorite.

It's comparable to:

"Life was lived fully"

"Action was taken"

"Stagnant air was repulsed and subsequently thrown away."

"Feet were awoken and rejoiced to the equation of a melody."

"Stillness was not taken as an answer."

But I think you just meant

"We moved the furniture around a bit and we're not finished."

I think I like my interpretation better.

SUNRISE/SET

Can you tell the difference

Between a sunrise

And a sunset?

Between the promising hope of a new adventure,

And the satisfying close of a book?

The hues are from the same paintbrush

Just drawn with different intentions

If I showed you a picture,

Could you tell me the difference?

Is it like a glass half-full/half-empty question?

Have you witnessed enough of either

To be able to tell the difference?

To be able to tell apart the hues

Of a sunrise and sunset.

I plan to witness enough of both.

And will probably tell you

That the difference is not in the hues

But in the feelings conjured,

The people close by,

The smells,

How the moment feels.

I want to be able to live in the moment so closely

That I can tell a sunrise

From a sunset.

BACK TO AUGUST

If you were to ask me

If I had feelings leftover

I would tell you

That that question

Isn't a yes or no question

And that scientists are still trying to prove

If feelings exist

That feelings

Aren't ontologically valid

And you would marvel

At my use of 'ontologically'

While I got away

Before you noticed

My lack of answer

I READ

I read

With prayer as bookends

"Love the Lord Your God with all your heart…"

I read

To grow in my faith

I read

To improve my vocabulary

So I can later impress a cutie

I read

To enter a world I wouldn't have – couldn't have – dreamed up myself

It's a much cheaper way to travel than real-world traveling

I read

To gain perspective; to hear the thoughts of others

Because once you hear the inner monologue of another person, you start to hear your own a little more clearly

I read

For quantity

"I read 14 books this summer, you?"

I read

For quality

To gain knowledge

I read

To understand life a little better

I read

For that feeling of satisfaction and longing to begin again after you slowly close a book

I read

TEACH THEM TO DANCE

To give and rejoice

Because life is lived best

When living for others

We were meant to live alongside each other

And nothing embodies joy more

Than a body in time to music

A joy so bright

Everyone in the room can see it

CRUX OF CHRISTIANITY

Love yourself

So that you may love others

Unconditionally

The way He loved us

SELF-CONSCIOUS IN A LIBRARY

I walk in

To a library

Do I fit?

I mean, will the avid readers notice that I haven't dropped by in months?

Will first-timers view me as a seasoned library connoisseur?

Just casual thoughts but

Why do we put ourselves into boxes?

For some reason this library makes me acutely aware of my appearance

Maybe I've been reading in third person for too long

Or maybe I haven't had enough human contact

But I'm dressed way too cute to be in a library

(Aren't library nerds supposed to be oblivious to name brands?)

And I have scrapes and bruises up my legs

Which would point to an adventurous lifestyle

Like maybe I went hiking, or cliff jumping

(Which is kind of funny because I did just go cliff jumping last night, but that's beside the point)

And aren't cliff jumpers too adventurous for libraries?

Although I did get these scrapes from falling up the stairs

Before I got to the first step

Clumsy people belong in libraries, right?

So many ideas

Of who belongs where

I think we put people into boxes

So it's easier to avoid the bad ones

SAVING MEMORIES

Some moments you savor

Because you know somewhere deep down – you just know – you'll need it later

Late evening at a best friend's house

Homemade pasta and the absence of turmoil of the constant sibling bickering

At this place there are no deadlines

The only responsibility you have is to share this meal with a friend

A rare and comforting peace

But then also

At home with the soundtrack of familiar voices

They've discovered your old music box

So you sit and drink in the sounds and the coffee

Hoping that by closing your eyes, concentrating

You'll be able to hear it better, longer

So you can remember it better, later

THE IMPORTANCE OF EATING WITH OTHERS (OR: THE EFFECT CUTE GUYS HAVE ON YOU)

My freshman year at college

This guy I had a crush on

Told me the importance of sharing meals with others

I thought it was so profound

I even included a paragraph or two about it

In an essay I wrote for an entry-level English class

I remember being frustrated because

I couldn't fully articulate

Why it's so important

I think there is truth to it

But back then

I just think I thought he was cute

THE ACTUAL IMPORTANCE OF EATING WITH OTHERS

At a primitive level

Sharing food shows trust

Care, acceptance, respect

But also it says,

"Let's pray together"

"I have time for you"

"Tell me about your day, even with all the frivolities,

because the frivolities are my favorite, heck, they're the reason I sat down"

I mean

There's got to be a reason

Why Jesus had a last supper

And not a last meeting

Why the Greeks had home-coming feasts

Why the Spaniards have multiple hour meals

Why neighborhood cookouts exist

And why fights and tension are so awkward at the dinner table

It's a place of peace

An unspoken, universally acknowledged nod to safety, familial territory

Sharing culture, a way to live

A way to stay alive

Sharing meals, that is

ON WHY I'M UP THIS LATE

Sometimes I stay awake

To keep tomorrow from happening

Pushing back the presence of the next day,

Like a child hanging on to a parent's leg,

Hoping to hold them back.

(the world moves fast when you're in an unconscious slumber

It's sneaky that way)

I always thought of night as extra time;

Anything I did that wasn't sleeping was a bonus.

I'm not done with today, yet.

I haven't done enough.

I didn't do everything I was supposed to

And it wasn't perfect. Let me start over.

Let me start over.

MAN IS SMALL

Ah I am deeply enthralled and satisfied and enjoy the thought

Of something being full when it physically can't be filled

The physical size being emphasized

Even when there is no size; when the 'something' is just an arbitrary idea

Or even better: a state of being

Death being full

And then to contrast this brilliant statement

With a truth so easily forgotten, because we like to turn our backs to it

Pretend it's not there

We're frail and easily succumb to death

Full of anguished and plangent cries

Or of equanimity and peace, looking forward to eternity

With a loving God

JUNE

And just like that, summer's gone

I bid thee, farewell

With a song

Of human alarm clocks

In the cute variety

Unpaid internships

That stress-jerk you awake

A sudden illness

Before the morning of the biggest test

Meaningful talks on the sidewalk with father

As tea parties and adventurers carry on

Lots of ponies and never enough playtime

Endless hours of staring at screens

Crafting, painting, building

Clocked hours at a pool that you can't jump in

But the people around are entertaining enough

"Yes, sir" "No, ma'am" "F*** that" "Language, Trevor. There are kids around."

Reconnecting with an old friend by putting mileage in our shoes

Friends: late-night-stalking laughter-inducing call-at-2am-in-tears-no-judgements kind of people

The ones who carry around the best moments in their pockets and

Gently plant them in your palm right when you need them

Cliff jumping and two-stepping and Reunion tower and first dates

Broken cars and thunderstorms right when you need to pray

Stopped cars and clouds of tears when you didn't expect them

"I have better for you"

Come, know me. Draw me nearer to You. Thank You.

Thank You. Thank You.

Fall

WAVES

God, why does it still hurt?

his name is too familiar to my tongue

And I wished I wasn't so used to it

Because the sea salt never quenches.

You were not a rip tide,

But a swelling of a giant wave

Overcoming the shore.

Why am I always surprised,

By how much it hurts when you inevitably crash back?

I rearranged my spaces

To make room for new thoughts

You seem to find your way into those, too

I wished the waves to stop

But they continued to crash onto my shore

A DRAMATIC RETELLING OF MY EARRING HOLDER BREAKING

First by threes

Then by fours

An unwelcome tragedy

But then again; aren't all tragedies unwelcome?

The first time, I thought to make it new

To mend, repair, just like before

When life gives you lemons...

The second time was thicker, fuller

A bang that slices through the stillness

It's worse at night, when you're buried under three layers of unconsciousness

Being dragged up through each layer.

So the second time I let the pieces sit

Thinking it must be a metaphor for something

For what, I know not quite yet

THE LUCKY CHARMS DILEMMA

Do I indulge myself and eat the marshmallows all at once,

From the beginning?

Only to be left with all the wooden parts...

No.

Or shall I savor them for the end?

It takes a lot of patience

And time.

Sometimes my mornings offer neither of those things.

So then shall I eat the marshmallows as I receive them?

Eating them as they come by the random spoonful?

Enjoying them as they present themselves?

But isn't that how everyone eats their lucky charms?

Blindly eating from their bowl, taking no note as to what they're about to enjoy next

Not everyone ponders the technique in which they will eat their cereal

The wooden parts to marshmallow ratio is a serious thing

I don't want to be just like anyone else.

PUZZLE

I think sometimes

I focus so much on being a good listener

That I don't know how to be a good talker

I forget where to look,

When to gesture my hands,

How to fluctuate my voice correctly.

I have two modes: serious & silly

Sometimes I don't feel genuine when I have to quickly switch between the two

Is it possible to feel genuine when you don't know who you are yet?

I'm still putting the pieces together,

Even though I have the picture on the box

Labelled: **Child of God**

A ROOM

There is a room

With an unplayed piano

Flowers wilting

A stale odor sits and makes its home there

A thick stillness

A silence so loud it makes you want to scream

Shake the foundation of the house

Take a hammer to the walls

Just so you can start over.

Some days,

I feel like that room.

Other days,

I feel like that room

When music filled between the walls; from floor to ceiling

Full to the brim

Colors exaggerated

So much movement that you can't breathe but

You know you must be breathing or how else could you feel so alive

And it's funny to say I feel like a room

Because rooms don't feel

But they do have a feeling

And it's funny to say I feel like the same room

Because geographically, that room is the same

But time changes it

And some days I wish I had more visitors

And other days I wish there were less

But at least I've gotten friendly with the termites

And the exterminator

I'm used to the pattern of the sunrays on my floor

The way the floor creaks about two feet over that way

The sounds of familiar footsteps approaching;

The gentle exhale of the opening door

That's my favorite because

I love being able to guess who is coming inside

RAINY DAYS

Rainy days are like the Sabbath.

Rest, peace, pitter patter

Magnifying the warmth you feel

By the contrasted cold

Comfort, safety, tap tap tap

Watching the vertical drops

Can be mind-numbing or stimulating,

Depending on which type of person you are;

Watch long enough and they look like they're falling up.

The rhythmic raindrops my favorite lullaby

The thunder reminds me I'm safe

The lightning: "LOOK!

Look at all there is!"

I've played in the rain

But now it's someone else's turn.

And why is it that rain makes moments more emotional?

Is it because we associate falling water with tears, and with tears, emotion?

A run, a dance, a hug

A confession, a reunion, a stoic contemplation

All more dramatic in the rain

I blame Hollywood

And love it all just the same

FACES

I hate that even hours after I'm finished crying

There are after effects on my face

Swollen eyes

Puffy cheeks

Creases on my brow

Emotion that swelled from my heart

Spilled onto my face

And dyed it some new color

Do it enough and you turn a new shade of you

And it's not just crying, either

Each emotion leaves its own signature souvenir;

Joy: little familiar folds around the mouth and eyes

Anguish: empty eyes

Curiosity: raised eyebrows

Burdened: an impressive forehead

Lost trust: puckered lips

Sum it up and you get your face

I watch faces and read what they've been through

You can tell a lot about a person's story by the colors it's been painted

And the remnants left on their face

SCRAP PAPER

I write meaningful words on scrap pieces of paper.

Like an artist whose medium is sand;

The product is all the more meaningful because of how quickly it can be blown away

Even in our bodies the most meaningful information,

DNA, is the most fragile.

Appreciate each for what it is, in that moment.

A word scratched out there.

A smooth curve in the grain.

An amino acid exchange.

A subtly-changing masterpiece.

And realize that

You

Are one, too

Changing slightly every moment

Being molded by memories and weather

And I think I write on scrap paper

Because it makes it more significant

SLOTH VIA GLUTTONY

I nibble at time like it's an endless supply

My flesh growing thicker with each heavy swallow

Warm and prickly

And as the time shrinks I get bigger

Dizzy from the fumes this flavor of time imposes

Before I know it time has run dry

I'm left with an empty head and weak ankles

CHANGE

What happens when my flowers are replaced with fake ones?

They do the trick, but

I know the difference.

IT IS

Well love,

Love is knowing when to say goodbye.

When to swallow your tears and put the photographs away in a box marked 'past' and not look at them until they become memories.

Love is knowing when to speak.

When to deliver difficult words no one else will say and when to ask for forgiveness and when to wrap a person around the words 'it will be OK'

And notice my dear that all of these things are never easy

Because, well, love is never easy.

If it were, it'd be called fun,

And while love can be fun

The fullest kind is never simply a three lettered word.

THE LORD

I smile

When a verse in the Bible ends with:

"I am the Lord."

Rapid, staccato, dramatic,

As if God needs to emphasize His power.

PLASTIC SURGERY SOCIAL MEDIA

I think there is a strong,

Direct correlation,

Between those who frequently use social media

And those who can't see themselves.

Or if they do see themselves,

They don't like what they see.

They use twitter as an airbrush,

Facebook as Botox,

Instagram as augmentation.

Fluffing up a life so much it's unrecognizable,

Even pathological.

Desperate

To figure out who they are

By allowing the world to tell them.

CONSTRUCTION (A POEM)

There's construction out my window.

As you can clearly see.

And while they're being productive,

The work is bothering me.

See I'm not against improvements

Nor change of any kind.

But I am against lights

That leave me feeling blind.

And I oppose constant racket

And men who whistle high

Then I get annoyed

While covering every inch of thigh

See I used to view a sky

Dotted with a cloud or two

Now in its place is dust

A film of a darker hue

And the smells aren't all that pleasant

Won't begin to ask why

I'll just keep my window shut

To what would've been the sky

There's construction out my window,

Listen with your ear.

Now I'm not against construction,

Just please don't do it here.

NOW

Now...

Well now I sing the melodies.

Whereas before was exclusively harmonies.

I learned to feel with each breath

To time every mood with each rhythm

To pause when you need to hear the silence

Because without silence

The music wouldn't sound so beautiful

CROWN OF JOY (NEHEMIAH 8:10)

For my 22nd birthday

We went and listened to a swing band

Outside at dusk.

And I made myself a crown of ivy

And thought about how it was such a 'Lauren-thing' to do.

My name means 'crown of joy'

I've always loved that.

(When I was younger I imagined a crown that imparted joy to the wearer and viewers alike)

I love the joy, part, mostly

Because it's such a wonderful, succinct emotion.

But then I got to thinking about the crown part,

Not only royalty,

But all-encompassing.

Joy that encircles like a crown

That exists not only in the small corner of happiness,

But in the large realm of being.

A joy that exists

Even in despair

Because it originates

From the Lord

Waiting to be chosen,

And each time it's picked

It's a victory.

Too often we reserve joy for when we think we've earned it.

Why would we allocate, or even worse, deny ourselves of joy

When it brings such good to our lives?

Sometimes, with benchmarks like a 22nd birthday,

We're reminded of the things we haven't achieved,

Of the people who have done so many great things at this age, or younger

Is that why people hate birthdays?

Because we're not as famous or rich or accomplished or as passionately in love as we thought we were going to be?

Do we hate birthdays because

The image of who our past-self thought we were going to be

And who we actually are

Rarely line up?

And on my 22nd birthday I decided

That I would ignore those thoughts of dissatisfaction

Those thoughts of unfulfillment

Or loneliness

Disappointment.

No. I would choose joy.

I will choose joy when joy is furthest away.

When it's left the grasp of my fingertips

I will choose joy when I get caught in routine.

I will choose joy when I feel I don't deserve it.

I will choose joy because others need it.

We have to consciously, constantly, actively choose

An all-encompassing joy.

And I will no longer wonder

When the good old days were or will be

Because I will live every day

As if they were the good old days

And joy will follow me there.

LIKE FROM THE PAGES OF A ROMANCE NOVEL

I do things like a character from a novel

Namely, a romance one.

I pretend that I'm doing it for myself,

But I'm doing it for the boy who's watching

The one who's supposed to fall in love with me

For doing small things like wearing an X-men tee out in public

Or potting a cactus in a teacup

Or not cursing

Or walking with confidence

Or reading with a flower in my hair

And he's the one who's supposed to notice these little things

And fall in love with me

And I'm the one "oblivious" that these are the reasons why.

One boy fell for it.

He fell for the character I was portraying.

I was afraid one day he'd figure out the real me

The raw, flawed, broken, eager, genuine, me.

That he'd open the box, assemble all the parts, and be disappointed with what he held.

He'd blame it on false advertising.

The girl he fell in love with

Was just one from a story

Who tried too hard to do things

That would make a boy fall in love with her

When he thought she wasn't watching.

She wasn't watching, but she was acutely aware,

How could she not be?

She was the one who orchestrated it all.

Of course, she wouldn't dare watch.

Falling in love is such a private moment.

One that's only allowed to be seen

When the other person doesn't know you're watching it happening.

No

Falling in love is a scary, fragile thing

When you decide that a person is worth caring about

That they now have a hold of a piece of you

And with it, a power to hurt you,

But an even greater power to give you hope.

The moment you fall in love with someone

Is private for that moment, but not for a moment longer.

And it should not be orchestrated

Or timed

Or stolen from the pages of a romance novel.

And it should happen without the
reserves of a warranty on the box.

WORDS

I like succinct words

Because in their distilled nature

They tell you everything they aren't

ALSO

It's funny how the people you come in contact with,

Leave a residue.

Which makes me wonder:

Are we just a sum

Of those we've collided with the most?

POEMS

The thing I like about poems

Is that

You have to slow down to read them

AND SO IT GOES

When did I stop becoming the person you called

Whenever you wanted to talk out an idea?

When did you stop telling me

About the things that make you happy?

How did we get to this point

Where I don't know what's going on anymore?

I don't like not knowing

What's going on anymore.

I thought…

But it doesn't matter.

That's life.

And so it goes.

FOR THE FIRST TIME SHE WAS HEALTHILY HUNGRY

To be healthily hungry

A signal, a feeling, that you've been out living

Being

And now you need fuel to continue living, being

The best kind of emptiness

Not enough to cause pain

Enough to show that

You exist; you function; you have a purpose

A literal emptiness that signifies a life lived full

A deep feeling, almost welcoming

Because the hungrier you are

The sweeter the taste

DAWN COLORED

Beginning

Bursts of color

Every shade and in between

An imperceptible movement

The rosy fingers of dawn

Grasping the globe

Greeting the morn

Gently

'hello'

ROUTINE

I was reading my favorite childhood book,

When I remembered why it was my favorite childhood book.

Our hero explains, as she searches for her enchanted prince that is currently a polar bear,

That magic cuts the processes of things.

It gives immediate satisfaction.

To be human is to be without magic.

Therefore, to be human is to go through processes.

Which is why, she realized,

She continued to do laundry when stuck in a castle.

Because routine is what keeps us human.

Routine is what keeps us sane.

The processes are where we find ourselves

We measure our strength how long we persevere

Our growth is made from mettle

Memories made from these moments

She was homesick for her blisters

And knew her magic bear would give up anything for that pain

MEANINGFUL

I have a friend

Who named her camera after a type of cannon (the weapon)

Because it was a Canon (the camera)

We should all live like that:

Putting thought into what we do

Giving meaning to the smallest of things.

It makes life worthwhile.

MY LOVE CUPPED IN MY HANDS

I measure my frustrations out in teaspoons

Letting them dissolve in my morning cup of peace

I keep my joy in my breast pocket

To give away so freely

Preserving my strength in jars

Because you'll never know when you need it

Planting my hope in the front garden

To let them know it's not all lost

I tuck away my fears between the pages of that book

Cracking it open when I need a reality check

And place my trust in the walls of my home

A sturdier foundation than I could ever build myself

2 CORINTHIANS 5:17

Chaos:

Steal, kill, destroy;

The point at my life when my flowers wilted.

And they had been dead for a while,

When a single

white

bud appeared.

New growth.

A small miracle.

Hope

Amidst chaos.

Strength

Amidst turmoil.

Even when surrounded by death,

There will be new creation.

"Behold, He has made a new creation.

The old has passed

The new has come."

Winter

CAN'T SLEEP

Late nights

Are the neon welcome sign for old memories,

A soft nod and a soothing voice that says, "go ahead"

Beckoning to

Thoughts you wouldn't normally let in.

There's something about the lack of sun

That makes us think thoughts that shouldn't transverse our mind.

And when the morning comes,

They shrink away with daylight,

Only to come back again,

On another late night.

WHAT IT'S LIKE TO GET OVER SOMEONE

First, it sucks.

This is not what you wanted.

And then it sucks,

Because it is what you wanted,

And you know you can never go back.

PRAYER

Lord,

I trust you.

Wholeheartedly.

In every aspect.

Forgive me for my weaknesses.

Let your power be made perfect by them.

Explore my heart, every crevice.

Know me.

Leave no stone unturned,

So that I may be perfectly vulnerable before you.

Guide me.

Use me.

Lead me.

I am here.

Here I am.

Your joy is unshakable

Your peace, unfathomable

Your love, unending

As I step out into this next chapter of my life

I pray you would be with me

And keep me moving.

I praise you for the blessings and struggles You've given me

Who knows what is yet to come

Amen

ON LOSING SOMEONE

Like water cupped in my hands

I naïvely tried to hold on

But you found ways to trickle through my fingertips

RAINER MARIE RILKE

"He remained a poet

Even when he washed his hands"

I want the same to be said of me

In that I remained a poet

A daughter

A big sister

A student

A woman

A servant of Christ

Even amidst the mundane

That I stayed consistent

Genuine

True to myself

Where most people overlook and get caught up in routine

I continue to make each moment my own

I leave my mark

So when people remember me

I won't be defined by what I've done

But by how I've done it.

OBSOLETE

I think everyone's biggest fear

Is that it's all pointless.

That our life means nothing

And subsequently, why bother living

That's what drives people to God

Or away from Him.

IDIOT

Idi/o- the root combining form meaning to not be known

In ancient societies, if you weren't involved,

And no one knew who you were,

You were an idiot.

You were not known.

And you did not know.

The connotation has changed a bit but

The humanness stays the same.

We were built to be known.

UNKNOWN

In the thesaurus

'humble'

Is a synonym

For 'unknown'.

I humbly disagree.

LADY FROM SPAIN

I take rosebuds as my entitled form of payment.

Drink their liquor 'til it's dry

And then do it all again

You have, of course, heard of me.

The woman who creates constellations out of daydreams

And memories out of cravings.

Pulling them from your brain like

How the wind pulls at your scarf

I button up my insecurities, tie them up with a bow, and hold them in close

Keeping me cold

While your two-way mirror reads 'warm'

I sing love songs to keep me from loving

You listen to keep from having to hear

And all the while we'll keep pretending

That what I'm doing means something

To either of us.

Indulge yourself little longer

I've got quite the appetite.

SHIPWRECK

Remember the time

We visited the museum?

I looked at the paintings

And you looked at me.

RENEWAL

It's amazing the renewal God will bring

Right when you need it.

My heart rests in His alone

My identity is no longer formed by what they will think

I find joy in myself by being myself

By being a creation of God

And acting as such

Existing as a prelude to the glory that will be revealed

Lord, thank you.

For freeing me of the chains of remorse

For opening my eyes to see

My actions aren't end all, be all

That You are greater

And I am more satisfied than I will ever be

When I'm with You

CHRISTMAS SONG

Because we're all just kids

And "Merry Christmas's" should always be given

Repetition never an issue

Neither is price

And you're only an adult

Until you hit ninety-three

LOVE IS ON ITS WAY

How comforting

To know that love is never truly lost

It is just away

IMPARTING GOOD

How beautiful

That the noise of another person

So joyful and melodious

Can bring life to another

That someone can be so familiar

That their joy is not only shared and reciprocated

But blossoms and multiplies and creates

How beautiful

That your laugh

Can make someone feel warm,

Safe.

Good.

And you did that.

You imparted goodness.

WRITING

Writing clears my head

Because it forces me to think

In complete thoughts

Everyday life only requires halfway thoughts.

In fact, it is the easier way to live life.

However, it's better to live with full thoughts.

Living life thinking it all in.

Paying attention to what makes you happy

And making each moment meaningful.

I read this poem

About how we keep waiting to live life

About how we idly let each day pass

Giving bored glances to each day

And then hoping we get more of them.

How ungrateful.

The poet brilliantly compares days to people;

We only really remember the truly beautiful or horrible ones.

I want to live each day with a clear head and appreciate each one,

So I will write.

I mustn't forget to write.

WITH GOD

Lord, allow me to trust in you.

I want to dwell in your presence so deeply that every action of mine is synchronized with your character.

That my words would replicate your melody.

That my actions would be a vessel for your light.

That I would be so in cahoots with You that our delights would be the same.

Our wills aligned.

That You would radiate from myself so others would find themselves on a path directed toward you.

When I am alone, I will turn to You so I will not be lonely.

When I am afraid, I will turn to you for peace.

When I am worried, I will turn to You for wisdom.

I want to walk with You not for manipulation for personal gains, but so that I may gain peace to successfully do Your work here on Earth.

Lord, lead me, even when I don't want to be led. I trust you.

In Jesus' name I pray,

Amen.

SINGING IN THE CAR

Gosh, some songs get to you.

That swelling, warm feeling

Building inside of you

When a familiar song imposes on your ears

Sometimes I'm all but happy when it plays but

I can't help but smile every time.

Sing loudly

Sometimes badly

Let your mouth open wide and smile big

Let the windows down so your arm gestures can be as wide as you need them to be

Perform for the people who aren't absorbed enough in other things

Perform for yourself

Because sometimes you need to be the person on the stage

Just don't forget to invite others up there with you

Sing loudly

Smile proudly

Lungs working

Growing stronger

And healthier

Breathing out the daily stresses

And in the music of the song that makes you smile when you don't want to

TRAINING

Lord, I'm afraid

Of being alone.

Of not experiencing romantic love.

The Lie I am told is

That if I'm consumed by You,

I will have nothing left to give someone else.

Or that my eyes will be closed to someone else.

Or that my calling will be to no one else.

What an interesting Lie I am told,

In order to be pulled further away from you.

I believed it, for a bit.

But now I am training myself.

Training to not fall into that trap.

My exercises include abstaining from sessions of wallowing in the past

Praying constantly

Singing when I don't want to

Until I want to

Turning to you when I am alone so I will not be lonely

Finding comfort in friends when I think there is deficiency in loyalty or 'being-with-peopleness'

Training my thoughts to find contentment in You

In singleness

And pushing away the longing of the idol of the coveted 'relationship'

That the word 'relationship' would no longer be coveted

Or idolized

But seen in the realistic perspective light of God

As a gift

That isn't always perfect

And that takes work

I'm in training

I get sore in the mornings

After a long workout

But it's a good sore

And I pray

For a lot of things but

I pray for my future husband.

I pray that he's working out, too.

HANDBOOK FOR LIFE

Speak in sonnets

Dance in harmonies

Cry in fugues

And sleep

In a sighed and gentle

'hallelujah'

GARDENING

No, it would be too simple to say

Gardening is a metaphor for life.

More like an instruction book

Or a miniature model set.

Water yourself and others

Pull out the weeds,

But make sure to get the roots,

Otherwise they come back twice as fast.

Endurance and hard work make for fruits.

Fruits take patience and time

And shouldn't be kept to ourselves.

You mustn't be afraid to get dirty

For in the soil you will be enriched.

SELF-AWARENESS TURNED BLEAK

Sometimes I get so caught up in my own self-reflections

That I forget to look up

I get caught up in learning how I think life should be lived

That I don't live it

I spend so much time trying to figure out who I am

That I forget who I was

I over-analyze and get de-sensitized

Or more sensitized

I become so introspective

That I forget to seek new perspective

It feels like I'm making progress

But I'm actually just becoming stagnant

And obsessive

Doing the kind of worry-work that gets you nowhere

Lord, teach me how to live freely

Being self-aware, but not self-absorbed

LET IT BE

Lord,

Prepare my heart for this next chapter

Let my faith be my own, and not my line of study

Let my relationships be beautifully flawed and broken

So that I don't place the pressure of perfection upon them

And so that Your glory may shine through those weaknesses

Let my laugh be genuine and my own

Let my arms be ready to catch those falling

And let my body be ready to fall

So those around will have the chance to catch me

Let my lungs be greedy

Taking in new kinds of air from new places

And inhaling too much from full laughs

Let my eyes have clarity

To see those hurting

And to see Your plans for me

Let my hands be comforting

And create things for Your glory

Let my feet be humble

And always ready to be guided

Let my heart be open to others

And ready for when he comes

Let my mind be at rest

And trust You with every bit of being

Lord, let these things be.

Amen.

WHAT IMPARTED

And if there's one thing that you've learned from me

I hope it's that you've learned to walk slower

And enjoy the cold

Because it's not just a "Lauren-thing"

Spring

HUMANITY

We can hear smiles

In songs

MY MOM

Mom learned to get ready quickly

Because she spent most of her mornings

Getting us kids ready first

She learned how to hide greasy hair

For the days there wasn't time for herself

She listens for hours

And isn't offended when we don't ask about her day

Mom never talks about herself; I have to pull her stories out

The epitome of selfless

That was how she lived;

Leaving everything behind her fixed

And forgetting to check if she was broken

ON DOWNTOWN WACO

How strange to dine

With wind chimes in my ear

And rough bass rumbling, threateningly, down the street

I'm not sure which is more ominous

WHAT IS NEXT

Oh I felt so loved

By my Father and all those around

To declare my life for Christ

And they shared today with me

They shared the symbol of new life

And become a part of it

Oh, I felt so loved

Lord, for Your goodness and graciousness

That I could have hope and peace

In the strangest, most unknown part of my life

That I could have friends and encouragers

And the people there are a testament to the love I've given

Because I was first given Love

I'm proud of how I've lived my life

That I've allowed myself to let You work through me

I know this will be the consistent story:

I will pray, I will wait, You will work through me

Lord this opposite feeling of impending doom

Has stuck to my chest and makes me free

Death to the old life; LIFE to the new!

A new chapter is beginning and I feel the energy buzzing out of my fingertips

Lead me. I'm listening. I'm here.

Ready to go wherever you call me.

I completely trust that life with You is greater and more fulfilling than any life I can imagine.

I don't know what is next

But I know it's gotta be good

IRRESPONSIBLY RECITING MY POETRY

The words spilled from my mouth

And fell to the floor

And arranged themselves in a way

That a secret part of myself was

Now vulnerably bare

That only a few were meant to see

FEELING SORRY FOR PAST-SELF

To feel hurt

Remembering past pain

A memory of -

A conjured third emotion

Not from the same origin of the first pain

And not leftovers

But alive and present simply because

There was pain

GRADUATING

Mourning

Is the only true way to describe it

A loss

Of something just. So. Good.

Just because it's over

Doesn't mean there isn't gain

Letting go and being sad

Because the chapter ends

"how lucky I am

To have something that makes saying goodbye

So hard"

Crying because it was so good

And holding on to this feeling

Of impending goodness

That Mick calls "trust"

But trust is a verb

And this is a feeling

I think

It's just abiding

Lord I trust You

Your will be done

Summer

HEARTS REVEALED

Resurfaced dream:

Of coffee shops and pianos;

String lights and ambiance;

Donations to spread joy.

The low conversations in A flat

Where even casual onlookers understand how in depth,

How intimate,

How important,

These conversations (of fellowship/understanding/newness) are

By the nods,

The bodies pulling in towards one another over the table,

The presence of eye contact and absence of screens.

The music: the quiet canvas and foundation for this scenery

Urging those who step into it

To take off their armor,

And masks,

Let their hearts do the talking for a while.

This is my resurfaced dream.

And if it will not be my coffee shop,

It will at least be my home.

FROZEN DINNERS

I'm afraid to live my life like a frozen dinner;

Reminiscent of the real thing

Pretending to be gourmet and sometimes being content but

Never quite getting it right

Or never quite living it fully

Enough

FORTUNE COOKIE MOMENT

Those who don't heed advice

Are often those who need it the most

DESIGNED

The commercials droned on in the background

But the toilet paper slogan, "designed to be forgotten"

Clung to my ears

I'm sure that's how some of us feel

Designed, to be forgotten

And what an empty, lonely life that would be

Purposeless and dull

But we were not designed to be forgotten

We were designed to be known

We were designed to be loved

We were designed to walk alongside another person

To make music because a song was placed on our heart

To live intensely with others

To create because we can and our minds are overflowing

To sit, and be, with other people

We were not designed for monotony

Or monetary

Things

Hidden tears & unarticulated fears

No

We were designed to live life intertwined

Sharing open hearts to gentle hands

And I will not let you believe

That you were designed to be forgotten

TECHNOLOGY NOWADAYS

Soft 'pings' emanate from people

A gentle reminder to them

That someone cares

By another like

Retweet

Text

Comment

But if everyone emanates pings

The world becomes a louder place,

Full of people who think they are feeling love

That's only digital

NEW SITUATIONS

Exaggerating your qualities

Like a character in a pilot episode

So others will know which part you play

TWO SONGS

I stood there

Listening

To two songs

And how strange it was

To listen to two songs

At one time

One from this floor and one from the next

One song was so clear

And the other was present, but sounded as if I were listening from a dream

As if my mind were at odds:

And it was like existing between two radio stations,

Being inside a schizophrenic's head,

Standing in-between two dimensions -

Being on the cusp of one stage of life and

Almost in the other.

And I realized, that where I physically was at that moment

Also represented where I was in my path of life

JUST IN CASE

And so I left my computer open

For others to stumble on my words

And maybe find joy in them

ABOUT THE AUTHOR

Lauren is from Frisco, Texas and graduated from Baylor University in 2015. Instead of going to medical school like she planned, God led her to Seminary to study Biblical Counseling (Proverbs 16:9). Lauren enjoys singing, painting, playing piano, and simply being with people. She is living to bring glory to Him in everything she creates.

Disclaimer & Copyright Information

All of the poems contained in this book are original works from the Author, and unless otherwise noted, are attributed to Lauren K Rodriguez.

Cover illustration, book design and production
Copyright © 2015 by Lauren Rodriguez
www.TributePublishing.com

www.ingramcontent.com/pod-product-compliance
Lightning Source LLC
Chambersburg PA
CBHW020614300426
44113CB00007B/635